MW01178996

XTREME
RESCUES

SAVING
APOLLO 13

JOHN HAMILTON

UNITED STATES

A&D Xtreme
An imprint of Abdo Publishing
abdobooks.com

abdobooks.com

Published by Abdo Publishing, a division of ABDO, PO Box 398166, Minneapolis, Minnesota 55439. Copyright © 2020 by Abdo Consulting Group, Inc. International copyrights reserved in all countries. No part of this book may be reproduced in any form without written permission from the publisher. A&D Xtreme™ is a trademark and logo of Abdo Publishing.

Printed in the United States of America, North Mankato, MN.
092019
012020

Editor: Sue Hamilton
Copy Editor: Bridget O'Brien
Graphic Design: Sue Hamilton & Dorothy Toth
Cover Design: Victoria Bates
Cover Photo: NASA
Interior Photos & Illustrations: All images NASA except:
Alamy-pgs 14-15;
Getty Images-pgs 18-19 ;
Getty Images/Walt Disney Television-pgs 20-21;
Shutterstock-pgs 6-7.

Library of Congress Control Number: 2019941917
Publisher's Cataloging-in-Publication Data

Names: Hamilton, John, author.
Title: Saving Apollo 13 / by John Hamilton
Description: Minneapolis, Minnesota : Abdo Publishing, 2020 | Series: Xtreme rescues | Includes online resources and index.
Identifiers: ISBN 9781532190056 (lib. bdg.) | ISBN 9781644943533 (pbk.) | ISBN 9781532175909 (ebook)
Subjects: LCSH: Apollo 13 (Spacecraft)--Accidents--Juvenile literature. | Space flight to the moon--Juvenile literature. | Space vehicle accidents--Juvenile literature. | Space rescue operations--Juvenile literature. | Space shuttles--Juvenile literature.
Classification: DDC 629.45409--dc23

CONTENTS

NASA's FINEST HOUR

On April 11, 1970, Apollo 13 blasted off from NASA's Kennedy Space Center in Florida. With an earthshaking roar, the mighty Saturn V rocket rode a pillar of flame into the sky. The launch went well, but after only five minutes the mission's three astronauts encountered their first problem. The Saturn V's center engine shut down. Luckily, the remaining four engines lifted them safely into orbit.

Apollo 13 lifts off from Florida's Kennedy Space Center on April 11, 1970.

Apollo 13 was launched into space using a three-stage Saturn V ("Saturn five") rocket. It towered 363 feet (111 m) tall, nearly 60 feet (18 m) taller than the Statue of Liberty. It weighed 6.2 million pounds (2.8 million kg) fully fueled. The five massive engines together gulped up to 20 tons (18 metric tons) of liquid fuel per second.

Saturn V
363 FEET
111 METERS

Statue of Liberty
305 FEET
93 METERS

Even though one of the spacecraft's engines failed, it was able to leave Earth's orbit. The Apollo 13 astronauts settled in for a three-day journey to the Moon. What they didn't know was that disaster was about to strike. It would take all their courage and ingenuity, plus the brainpower of NASA's finest scientists, to get them safely home in their crippled spacecraft.

THE MISSION

Apollo 13 was NASA's third Moon-landing mission. Apollo 11 and 12 explored the Moon's flat plains, called *maria*. Apollo 13's mission was to explore part of the lunar highlands. These tall regions appear brighter to us on Earth. Two of the three astronauts were to land on the Moon and explore the highlands. They were trained to use scientific instruments to study the region's geology.

Astronauts Fred Haise (left) and Jim Lovell train to use geology instruments in Hawaii in 1969.

Gambart

0°
0°
−30°
−60°
+30°
+60°

S

Moon

Turne

The Moon's Fra Mauro area was Apollo 13's landing destination.

Fra Mauro

Rimae Parry

Parry

Bonpland

Tolansky

9

THE CREW

Jim Lovell,
Commander

In 1970, Commander Jim Lovell was the most-traveled man in history. Over the course of three missions, he had spent 572 days in space covering nearly 7 million miles (11.3 million km).

Apollo 13's other two crew members included command module pilot John "Jack" Swigert and lunar module pilot Fred Haise. Neither had flown in space, but they were both experienced pilots. Each had completed thousands of hours of astronaut training.

Jack Swigert,
Command
Module Pilot

Fred Haise,
Lunar
Module Pilot

XTREME FACT

The original Apollo 13 crew included command module pilot Thomas "Ken" Mattingly. However, he was exposed to German measles and replaced as a precaution three days before launch.

THE SPACECRAFT

The Apollo 13 spacecraft had three main parts, called modules. The cone-shaped command module was where the crew spent the most time. It had about the same amount of room inside as a large car. Behind the command module was the service module. It held fuel, electricity, plus scientific instruments. The lunar module was the part that would land on the Moon. It was built to hold just two astronauts.

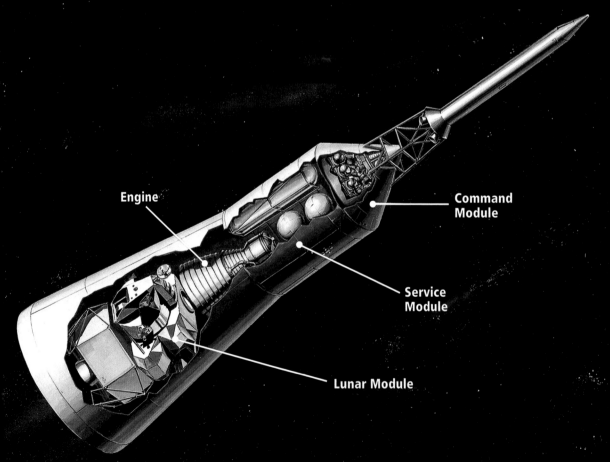

Engine

Command Module

Service Module

Lunar Module

A view of Apollo 14's lunar module on the Moon's surface. Astronauts called the lunar module, or LM, the "lem."

XTREME FACT

Apollo 13's command module was named Odyssey. The lunar module was named Aquarius.

EXPLOSION

About 2 days and 8 hours into the mission, Apollo 13's crew heard a loud bang. They felt the whole spacecraft shudder. Alarms and warning lights flashed. Electrical power began to drop. At first, the astronauts thought a meteoroid may have slammed into the spacecraft. Jack Swigert spoke on the radio to NASA's Mission Control in Houston, Texas. "Okay, Houston," he said, "we've had a problem here."

The explosion was caused by damaged wires. They were on a fan inside an oxygen tank in the service module. Earlier testing accidentally caused overheating inside the tank. The heat melted the insulation around the wires.

Nobody knew about the damage until the fan was turned on 56 hours into the mission. The bare wires sparked a fire. The oxygen-rich tank blew up with the force of a shotgun blast. The explosion damaged wiring, pipes, and valves.

Mission Control is packed with astronauts and flight controllers anxiously awaiting news from the damaged Apollo 13 spacecraft.

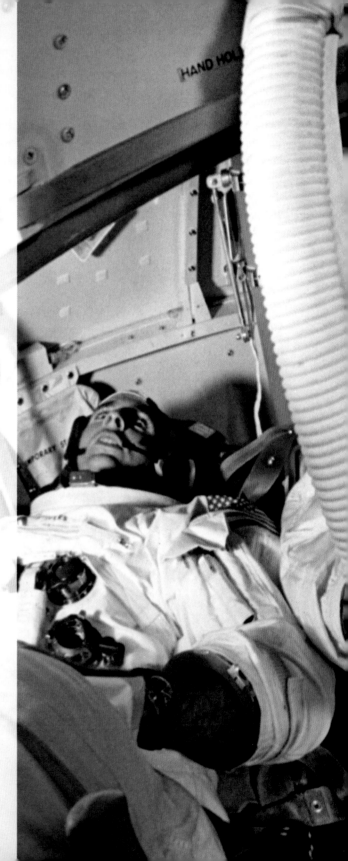

RESCUE PLANS

Unlike what happened in the movie *Apollo 13*, the astronauts did not argue about who was to blame for the explosion. They remained calm. Their only concern was the condition of the spacecraft and their own safety. Commander Lovell could see a cloud of gas venting into space from the side of the crippled spacecraft. He knew they were in deep trouble. They were more than 200,000 miles (321,869 km) from Earth.

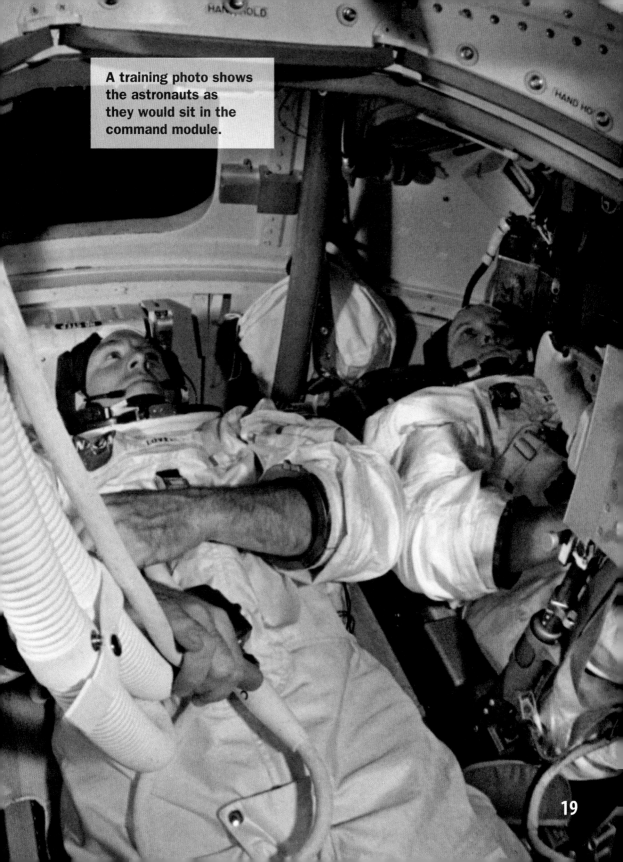

A training photo shows the astronauts as they would sit in the command module.

THE WORLD FINDS OUT

The explosion knocked out most of the command module's electricity, water, and heat. News of the astronauts' peril quickly reached the world.

The crew was forced to shut down electrical systems in the command module. They had to save whatever electricity was left or they wouldn't have enough power to land safely. Lovell, Swigert, and Haise moved into the lunar module *Aquarius* and used it as a lifeboat. They barely had enough oxygen, heat, and water to survive the long journey back to Earth.

Newscasters explain to the world the serious problems Apollo 13 faced.

AROUND THE MOON

As the astronauts hurtled through space, scientists at Mission Control in Houston worked tirelessly. They planned a way to get the crew home safely without running out of fuel. The astronauts were told to continue on course and fly once around the Moon. The Moon's gravity gave the spacecraft a "slingshot" boost back toward Earth. The astronauts fired their engine to make midcourse corrections. With help from Mission Control, they were soon on the right path home.

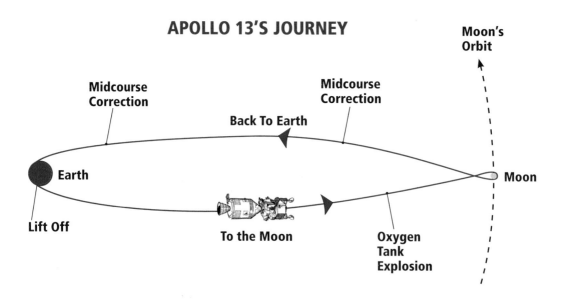

APOLLO 13'S JOURNEY

Moon's Orbit

Midcourse Correction

Midcourse Correction

Back To Earth

Earth

Moon

Lift Off

To the Moon

Oxygen Tank Explosion

The crew of Apollo 13 holds the record for traveling the farthest distance from Earth, approximately 248,655 miles (400,171 km).

XTREME FACT

A close-up photo of the Moon taken from the lunar module *Aquarius*.

Bad Air

Inside the lunar module, the crew's breathing was slowly causing carbon dioxide gas to build up. They ran out of canisters that helped "scrub" carbon dioxide out of the foul air. Spare cube-shaped canisters from the command module did not fit into the round hole of the air scrubber in the lunar module. Luckily, Mission Control invented a way for the astronauts to use plastic bags, hoses, a sock, and tape to make the canisters fit.

Director of Flight Crew Operations Deke Slayton shows NASA officials the device developed to "scrub" carbon dioxide out of the Apollo 13 lunar module.

Jack Swigert moves needed items into the lunar module lifeboat. Near his shoulder is the gray "mailbox" that they used to scrub the air of carbon dioxide.

XTREME FACT

Carbon dioxide can build up in a person's bloodstream in an enclosed area. This causes a dangerous condition called hypoxia. The brain can't get enough oxygen. It causes confusion, memory loss, and eventually death.

The astronauts see
the terrible damage to the
service module after it is released.

REENTRY

The astronauts suffered for several days with little to eat or drink, and with almost no sleep. They also endured freezing temperatures. Finally, they reached Earth on April 17, 1970. They moved into *Odyssey* and turned the power back on. They released the lunar and service modules, and then made a fiery descent through Earth's atmosphere. They splashed down safely in the Pacific Ocean. The entire world welcomed them home as heroes.

After a successful splashdown on April 17, 1970, the Apollo 13 astronauts wave as people around the world cheered their safe return to Earth.

What If It Happens To You?

How do you survive when you're stranded somewhere with little hope of rescue? The first rule is to not panic. That is exactly how the astronauts of Apollo 13 were trained, and it saved their lives. Panic prevents a person from thinking clearly. Keeping yourself calm will help you think of the best way out of a seemingly hopeless situation. All three astronauts and the entire staff of NASA worked calmly and tirelessly to bring them home safely. Failure was never an option.

Astronaut Jim Lovell reads a newspaper article about Apollo 13's safe return.

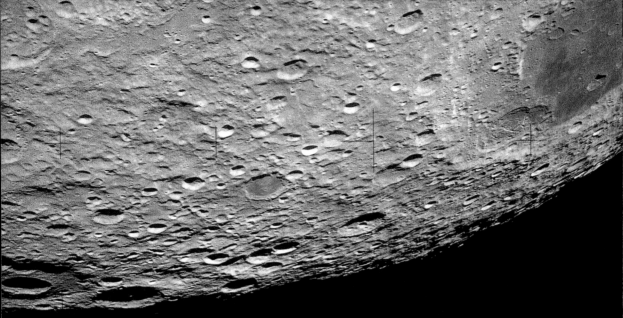

Glossary

Astronaut
Someone who travels in a spacecraft. The word has Greek roots that stand for "star sailor" or "star traveler."

Maria
The flat plains of the Moon. The lunar maria are huge regions made of basalt. They were formed by volcanic eruptions long ago. They appear as dark areas to observers on Earth. Maria is a Latin word that means "seas." The first astronomers mistook the dark regions for real oceans of water on the Moon.

Meteoroid
A meteoroid is a solid object, usually rocky, that moves through space. It is small, ranging from the size of a grain of sand to about one meter in diameter. If a meteoroid enters a planet's atmosphere, it becomes a meteor.

NASA (NATIONAL AERONAUTICS AND SPACE ADMINISTRATION)
A United States government space agency started in 1958. NASA's goals include space exploration and increasing people's understanding of Earth, our solar system, and the universe.

ORBIT
The circular path a moon or spacecraft makes when traveling around a planet or other large celestial body. For example, the International Space Station takes about 90 minutes to make one complete orbit around the Earth.

SPLASHDOWN
When a spacecraft lands in water instead of on dry land. Apollo spacecraft landed in the ocean—a splashdown.

STAGE
In order to fly as high as possible, some rockets have more than one section, called stages. Each stage has its own engine and fuel. They are stacked on top of each other. When the first stage runs out of fuel, it drops away and falls to Earth, or burns up in the atmosphere. The Saturn V rocket used three stages.

ONLINE RESOURCES

Booklinks
NONFICTION NETWORK
FREE! ONLINE NONFICTION RESOURCES

To learn more about saving Apollo 13, visit abdobooklinks.com or scan this QR code. These links are routinely monitored and updated to provide the most current information available.

INDEX

The lunar module *Aquarius* was released into space just before Apollo 13 reentered Earth's atmosphere.